Acknowledgement

This book was inspired by a number of conversations, including one with Emily. Those discussions helped surface the ideas explored here and prompted me to think about partnership in a different way.

Emily - Thank your for the encouragement and the great conversations that created the spark for this book.

Introduction

This book came out of a conversation.

I was walking through the ideas behind my earlier books, including how I've used the lunar cycle as a framework for understanding timing, focus, and what is needed at different points in a cycle. As part of that discussion, the topic turned to women's cycles and the similarities between the two.

The question that came up was simple: if a man has done work around self-awareness and self-regulation, does that help him better understand and partner with a woman as she moves through her own cycle?

Once the question was asked, the connection felt obvious. This book explores that connection and what it might look like in practice.

For the Women Reading This
This book is written from a masculine perspective, but it is not written *at* women. It is an attempt to reflect on how men can become more aware, more responsive, and easier to partner with.

If you've ever wished the men in your life understood timing, energy, or shifts in need more clearly, this book is written with that reality in mind.

For the Men Reading This
This book assumes you're willing to look at yourself honestly. It doesn't ask you to fix anyone or to manage someone else's experience. It asks whether awareness you've developed in your own life can translate into better partnership.

Table of Contents

Chapter 1

THE FOUNDATION WE'RE STARTING FROM

This book builds from three earlier works: The Divine Masculine Body, The Divine Emperor Within, and The Emperor's Journal.

The first book focused on outcomes related to embodiment and presence. At its core, it was about a man becoming more connected to himself and, as a result, more capable of connecting with others. The emphasis was on slowing down enough to feel what is actually happening in his body and in his relationships. From that place, a man develops a grounded sense of worth that is not dependent on external validation. He becomes more present, more communicative, and more capable of sensing what is happening with his partner rather than reacting automatically.

That work laid the foundation for a different way of relating. Not only to intimacy, but to life more broadly. A man who can feel is better equipped to listen, to communicate honestly, and to stay engaged without needing to control outcomes.

The second and third books introduced a complementary pillar. They explored the idea that timing matters. Through the framework of the lunar cycle, men were asked to recognize that growth, action, expression, reflection, and rest all have their place. The lunar phases provided a way to understand that not every moment calls for the same response.

Across those books, men were challenged to set intentions, take action when action was appropriate, reflect honestly, and grow through repeated cycles. The emphasis was not on constant effort, but on alignment with the moment.

When these two foundations are combined, something important emerges. A man who can feel, communicate, and be present, and who also understands that timing matters, is well positioned to engage in partnership with greater awareness. He is less reactive, less rigid, and more capable of adjusting how he shows up based on what is actually needed.

That is the foundation this book starts from.

The question this book explores is how those capacities translate into partnership with a woman who is moving through her own natural cycles. Not as something to manage or predict, but as something to meet with steadiness and understanding.

Chapter 2

A PRACTICAL RECAP OF THE LUNAR FRAMEWORK

The lunar cycle is commonly described in eight phases. In the books referenced above, these phases were used to orient awareness and intention rather than prescribe behavior.

The **New Moon** is associated with pause and reset. Outward momentum is reduced and attention naturally turns inward.

The **Waxing Crescent** phase follows, bringing early movement and the setting of intention. Direction begins to take shape, but energy is still building.

The **First Quarter,** often called **the half moon**, introduces effort and adjustment. Momentum meets resistance and refinement becomes necessary.

The **Waxing Gibbous** phase emphasizes patience and preparation. Energy continues to build, and attention often turns toward refinement rather than initiation.

The **Full Moon** represents expression and visibility. Energy peaks and what has been developing tends to show itself more fully.

The **Waning Gibbous** phase shifts toward integration. Experiences are processed and reflection becomes more prominent.

The **Last Quarter,** the **second half moon,** brings discernment and correction. This is where realignment and release often occur.

Finally, the **Waning Crescent** phase returns to rest and completion. Outward focus diminishes and space is created for the next cycle to begin.

Across these phases, men were asked to set intentions, reflect, act when appropriate, and grow through awareness of timing. The framework exists to support responsiveness rather than force.

Chapter 3

THE MENSTRUAL CYCLE
IN REAL TERMS

Biologically, the menstrual cycle is often described in four phases: menstrual, follicular, ovulatory, and luteal. While individual experience varies, these phases provide a useful structure for understanding how energy and needs tend to shift.

During the menstrual phase, energy often turns inward. Many women experience a greater need for rest, reduced stimulation, and quiet. Sensitivity can increase and the desire to withdraw slightly is common.

The follicular phase typically brings renewed energy and curiosity. Momentum begins to rebuild and engagement with the outside world often feels easier.

The ovulatory phase is often associated with outward expression, confidence, and connection. Energy tends to peak and visibility increases.

The luteal phase brings a gradual descent. Sensitivity, honesty, and discernment often increase as energy shifts inward again.

These changes are part of a repeating rhythm. Recognizing that rhythm helps prevent misinterpretation and unnecessary conflict.

Chapter 4

MENSTRUAL PHASE AND
INWARD LUNAR PHASES

Correlated Lunar Phases: New Moon and Waning Crescent

The menstrual phase is often experienced as a genuine turning inward. Energy drops. The nervous system seeks quiet. Many women feel a reduced tolerance for stimulation, conversation, and external demands. There is often a desire for rest, simplicity, and fewer expectations. This is not a withdrawal from relationship, but a physiological and emotional reset.

This phase aligns most closely with the New Moon and Waning Crescent phases of the lunar cycle.

In The Divine Emperor Within, the New Moon was framed as a phase of pause and reset. It was the moment when outward momentum was meant to stop. Men were asked not to initiate, not to advance plans, and not to push for clarity. The orientation was inward, reflective, and quiet. The outcome was learning how to remain present without movement.

The Waning Crescent completed the lunar cycle. It emphasized rest, release, and letting go of what had already run its course. Men were challenged to stop carrying energy forward simply because they could. The outcome here was learning how to rest without anxiety and release without disengaging from themselves or their lives.

Together, these lunar phases taught the man something fundamental: connection does not require activity.

That learning is directly relevant to supporting a woman during the menstrual phase.

When a woman's system turns inward, what she often needs most is the absence of pressure. Not the absence of presence, but the absence of demand. A man who has internalized the New Moon and Waning Crescent understands that inward movement is not a problem to solve. It is a phase to be respected.

Because the lunar framework taught him that rest is productive and that cycles must complete before they renew, he does not interpret reduced engagement as rejection. He does not escalate conversation to regain reassurance. He does not require emotional output to feel secure in the connection.

What he brings forward instead is steadiness.

This steadiness matters because it allows the woman's system to reset without having to manage his emotional state at the same time. She does not need to explain herself. She does not need to justify why she is quieter, less social, or less available. The relationship does not feel conditional on her energy.

What is commonly missed in this phase is misinterpretation. Men often read quiet as distance. They assume something is wrong. They push for clarity, reassurance, or engagement precisely when the woman's system is asking for less. Even well-intentioned concern can become pressure.

Another common miss is emotional over-correction. Some men withdraw completely, mistaking space for absence. The woman is then left feeling unsupported rather than rested.

What tends to work better is presence without intrusion. The man remains consistent. He checks in without expectation. He offers availability without insisting it be used. He stays grounded in himself rather than scanning for signs of approval or disconnection.

This is where the outcomes from The Divine Masculine Body also matter. A man who has learned to feel and regulate his own internal state does not rely on his partner's responsiveness to feel stable. He can sit in quiet without anxiety. He can remain connected without conversation. His presence feels calm rather than demanding.

For women, being met this way often feels deeply supportive. There is relief in not having to perform connection. There is safety in knowing the relationship remains intact even when energy is low. Trust grows because the man's steadiness is not dependent on her output.

This phase is foundational. When it is respected, the cycle moves forward more smoothly. When it is rushed or resisted, tension accumulates unnecessarily and often spills into later phases.

The menstrual phase does not require fixing. It requires patience, steadiness, and restraint. The lunar framework already trained the man in exactly those capacities.

Chapter 5

FOLLICULAR PHASE AND
EMERGING LUNAR PHASES

Correlated Lunar Phases: Waxing Crescent and First Quarter

The follicular phase begins after menstruation and is often experienced as a gradual return of energy and engagement. Curiosity increases. The body and nervous system begin to turn outward again. Many women feel more open to interaction, conversation, and possibility during this phase, though momentum is still building and not yet at full strength.

This phase aligns most closely with the Waxing Crescent and First Quarter phases of the lunar cycle.

In The Divine Emperor Within, the Waxing Crescent was the phase where intention was clarified. Men were asked to name direction without forcing outcome. Energy was present, but still forming. The outcome of this phase was learning how to hold intention lightly, without urgency or attachment to immediate results.

The First Quarter, the first half moon, introduced friction. Momentum encountered resistance. Men were challenged to stay engaged without becoming rigid. The outcome here was adaptability. Learning how to respond to obstacles without abandoning direction or escalating force.

Together, these lunar phases taught the man how to engage emerging momentum without overwhelming it.

That learning directly supports a woman during the follicular phase.

As a woman's energy begins to return, she may feel more communicative, curious, and outward-facing. At the same time, her system is still transitioning. Momentum is real, but it is not yet stable. A man who understands the Waxing Crescent and First Quarter does not treat this phase as a signal to accelerate everything. He recognizes that openness does not mean readiness for full intensity.

What he brings forward is encouragement without pressure.

Because the lunar framework taught him to set intention without forcing outcome, he does not rush the connection forward. He allows engagement to build naturally. Because he learned adaptability during the First Quarter, he remains flexible rather than rigid when plans shift or energy fluctuates.

What is commonly missed in this phase is pacing. Men often mistake renewed openness for full availability. Enthusiasm turns into urgency. Direction becomes expectation. What could have been supportive momentum becomes subtle pressure.

Another common miss is over-defining. Men try to name what things are becoming too early, rather than allowing space for exploration. This can collapse curiosity instead of supporting it.

What tends to work better is responsiveness rather than assumption. The man engages, listens, and participates without trying to steer the process. He shows interest without needing commitment to be declared. His presence communicates availability without demand.

This is also where the outcomes from The Divine Masculine Body matter. A man who has learned to feel and regulate himself does not project his excitement onto his partner. He remains aware of his own internal state and does not ask the woman to manage it for him.

For women, being met this way often feels freeing. There is room to explore without being directed. Curiosity is supported rather than captured. The relationship feels like a space of possibility rather than expectation.

When the follicular phase is respected, momentum builds cleanly. When it is rushed, tension often appears later, disguised as confusion or misalignment.

The follicular phase invites engagement, but not acceleration. The lunar framework already taught the man how to walk that line.

Chapter 6

OVULATORY PHASE AND
EXPRESSIVE LUNAR PHASES

Correlated Lunar Phases: Waxing Gibbous and Full Moon

The ovulatory phase is often experienced as a peak in outward energy. Confidence increases. Communication feels easier. Many women feel more expressive, socially engaged, and connected during this phase. There is often a sense of visibility, attraction, and openness that comes naturally rather than being effortful.

This phase aligns most closely with the Waxing Gibbous and Full Moon phases of the lunar cycle.

In The Divine Emperor Within, the Waxing Gibbous was the phase of refinement. Men were asked to stay attentive to what was developing without rushing toward culmination. The emphasis was on patience and care. The outcome was learning how to tend growth without trying to control its timing.

The Full Moon represented expression and visibility. Men were invited to step fully into presence, confidence, and connection without performance. The outcome was learning how to be expressive without escalation, and visible without needing validation.

Together, these lunar phases taught the man how to be fully present during moments of high energy without becoming overwhelming or self-focused.

That learning directly supports a woman during the ovulatory phase.

As a woman's energy peaks, connection can feel expansive and alive. There is often a natural desire for closeness, engagement, and shared experience. A man who understands the Waxing Gibbous and Full Moon recognizes that this openness does not require intensification or capture. He does not confuse expression with availability for constant engagement.

What he brings forward instead is grounded presence.

Because the lunar framework taught him to remain patient during growth and centered during expression, he can meet this phase without losing himself. He enjoys connection without needing to prolong it. He participates without trying to dominate the moment or extract reassurance from it.

What is commonly missed in this phase is overreach. Men mistake high energy for unlimited capacity. They escalate intensity, expectation, or attention in ways that can become subtly draining. What felt like openness begins to feel like demand.

Another common miss is performance. Men attempt to "match" the moment by doing more, saying more, or showing up bigger than necessary. This can shift the dynamic from mutual connection to imbalance.

What tends to work better is presence without inflation. The man remains engaged, attentive, and expressive, but he stays rooted in himself. He allows enjoyment to be shared rather than consumed. He trusts that connection does not need to be maximized to be meaningful.

The outcomes from The Divine Masculine Body are essential here. A man who has learned to feel and regulate his own internal state does not rely on heightened connection to define his worth. He can enjoy closeness without clinging to it. His presence feels secure rather than needy.

For women, being met this way often feels affirming and energizing rather than overwhelming. There is space to express and connect without being pulled into managing the other person's intensity. The relationship feels mutual and alive.

When the ovulatory phase is met with grounding rather than escalation, it strengthens connection rather than exhausting it. The lunar framework already taught the man how to remain centered during moments of peak energy. Ovulation is often associated with outward expression, attraction, and connection. Energy peaks and engagement becomes more visible.

This phase draws correlation from the Waxing Gibbous and Full Moon phases of the lunar cycle. These phases emphasize refinement and expression.

What matters most here is balance. Presence and confidence can coexist with restraint. Awareness allows connection to deepen without becoming overwhelming or misaligned.

Chapter 7

LUTEAL PHASE AND
INTEGRATIVE LUNAR PHASES

Correlated Lunar Phases: Waning Gibbous and Last Quarter

The luteal phase is often experienced as a gradual turning inward after the outward energy of ovulation. Sensitivity increases. Tolerance for misalignment tends to decrease. Many women notice a stronger need for honesty, clarity, and emotional truth during this phase. What was previously easy to overlook may now feel more present or harder to ignore.

This phase aligns most closely with the Waning Gibbous and Last Quarter phases of the lunar cycle.

In The Divine Emperor Within, the Waning Gibbous was the phase of integration. Men were asked to slow down and reflect on what had unfolded rather than rushing forward. The emphasis was on processing experience honestly, noticing what worked, what did not, and what was asking to be acknowledged. The outcome was learning how to integrate rather than bypass.

The Last Quarter, the second half moon, emphasized discernment and correction. Men were challenged to take responsibility for what was misaligned and to make adjustments without defensiveness or self-judgment. The outcome here was accountability paired with steadiness.

Together, these lunar phases taught the man how to stay present when clarity sharpens rather than withdraw or escalate.

That learning directly supports a woman during the luteal phase.

As a woman's system shifts toward discernment, she may feel less willing to smooth over discomfort or ignore what feels off. Honesty can become more direct. Emotional nuance may feel heightened. A man who understands the Waning Gibbous and Last Quarter does not interpret this shift as an attack or a problem to be shut down.

What he brings forward is listening without collapse.

Because the lunar framework taught him that reflection is a necessary part of growth, he does not rush to defend himself. He does not immediately try to fix, explain, or resolve everything. He understands that being present with truth is often more important than finding solutions in the moment.

What is commonly missed in this phase is mislabeling. Men often interpret discernment as criticism and sensitivity as conflict. In response, they become defensive, disengaged, or overly corrective. This turns a phase that could deepen understanding into unnecessary tension.

Another common miss is urgency. Men try to resolve discomfort quickly so they can return to a more comfortable dynamic, rather than allowing the phase to do its work.

What tends to work better is steadiness paired with openness. The man listens fully. He reflects rather than reacts. He acknowledges what he hears without immediately needing to justify himself. His presence communicates that honesty will not destabilize the relationship.

The outcomes from The Divine Masculine Body matter deeply here. A man who can feel and regulate his internal response is less likely to shut down when discomfort arises. He can stay embodied and engaged even when the conversation is not easy. His nervous system remains settled, which allows the exchange to remain grounded.

For women, being met this way often feels validating. There is space to speak honestly without fear of escalation or withdrawal. Emotional truth is received rather than resisted. Trust grows because the relationship can hold discomfort without breaking.

When the luteal phase is met with presence and accountability rather than defensiveness, it becomes a place of refinement rather than rupture. The lunar framework already taught the man how to stay engaged during moments of correction and clarity.

Chapter 8

WHERE THE CYCLES MEET

This side-by-side view is not meant to explain everything. It is meant to show pattern. When the cycles are looked at together, similar needs appear again and again: less fixing, more presence, clearer listening, and better timing. What is often missed is not awareness of the cycle, but how easily it is pushed aside in a relationship. The next chapter looks at where those misses show up and how they affect connection.

Menstrual Cycle Phase	Lunar Cycle Correlation		Core Correlations
Menstrual Phase	New Moon	Waning Crescent	• Energy turns inward • Rest, release, and reset are primary • Presence matters more than action • Space without withdrawal
Follicular Phase	Waxing Crescent	First Quarter Moon	• Energy begins to rise • Curiosity and openness return • Intention without pressure • Support growth, do not rush momentum
Ovulatory Phase	Waxing Gibbous	Full Moon	• Peak clarity and expression • Desire for connection and engagement • Mutual visibility and responsiveness • Show up fully without oversteering
Luteal Phase	Waning Gibbous	Last Quarter Moon	• Discernment and sensitivity increase • Need for honesty and refinement • Reduce friction, listen more than fix • Prepare for inward shift

Chapter 9

WHAT IS COMMONLY MISSED
ACROSS CYCLES

When partnership becomes strained, it is rarely because either person is fundamentally wrong. More often, it is because rhythm has been ignored. Cycles are happening whether they are acknowledged or not. When they are not understood, people begin reacting to shifts rather than responding to them.

One of the most common misses across cycles is personalization. Natural changes in energy, engagement, and sensitivity are taken personally. Inward phases are interpreted as distance. Outward phases are interpreted as obligation. Discernment is interpreted as criticism. Expression is mistaken for permanence. When these misinterpretations stack, unnecessary stories form.

Another frequent miss is timing confusion. Men often apply the same relational posture regardless of phase. They initiate when stillness would be more supportive. They intensify when presence would be enough. They seek resolution when reflection is actually needed. This mismatch creates friction not because care is lacking, but because the response does not fit the moment.

There is also a tendency to overcorrect. When men begin learning about cycles, some swing between extremes. They either disengage too fully in inward phases or over-involve themselves during outward ones. In both cases, the issue is not intention. It is calibration. Understanding cycles does not mean withdrawing or inserting oneself rigidly. It means staying connected without forcing alignment.

Another commonly missed element is expectation carryover. Energy from one phase is assumed to sustain into the next. When it does not, disappointment or confusion arises. This is especially true when outward energy is followed by inward movement. What felt open and expressive suddenly becomes quieter, and the shift is misread as loss rather than transition.

The final miss is failing to integrate embodiment with timing. Timing awareness without embodiment becomes intellectual. Embodiment without timing becomes reactive. The earlier books were explicit about this balance for a reason. A man must be able to feel what is happening in himself while also understanding what phase he is in. Without both, awareness collapses under pressure.

What becomes clear when looking across cycles is this: most relational strain is not caused by conflict, but by misalignment with rhythm. People push during phases that ask for patience. They withdraw when expression is actually supported. They react instead of observe.

When cycles are respected, the relationship does not become perfect, but it becomes more forgiving. Shifts stop feeling threatening. Discomfort stops being urgent. Expression stops feeling like a contract rather than a moment.

This chapter exists to name what repeatedly derails connection so it can be recognized earlier. Not judged. Recognized.

Understanding cycles does not eliminate challenge. It reduces unnecessary damage.

Chapter 10

WHAT CAN BE BROUGHT FORWARD

Once cycles are understood, the work is no longer about reacting correctly. It becomes about orientation. What a man brings forward into partnership matters less in how it looks and more in how it feels to be met by it.

The first thing that can be brought forward is steadiness. Steadiness is not passivity. It is the ability to remain emotionally available without needing the moment to confirm anything about one's worth or security. Across all phases, steadiness allows shifts to happen without destabilizing the relationship. It communicates that connection is not fragile.

Another essential quality is discernment without urgency. When timing is understood, discomfort does not immediately demand resolution. Questions can be held. Conversations can unfold over time. This creates room for honesty to surface without fear that it will break something. Discernment becomes a tool for refinement rather than a trigger for defense.

A third quality is responsiveness instead of assumption. When cycles are respected, a man stops assuming what engagement should look like and begins responding to what is actually present. This responsiveness keeps the relationship alive and adaptive rather than rigid. It allows both partners to stay current with each other rather than trapped in expectation.

Equally important is restraint paired with availability. Restraint does not mean withholding. It means knowing when not to act, not to push, and not to fill space unnecessarily. Availability remains constant, but it is not imposed. This balance supports trust across both inward and outward phases.

Another capacity that can be brought forward is emotional self-regulation. When a man has learned to feel and manage his internal state, he does not ask his partner to regulate it for him. This reduces pressure across all cycles. It allows each phase to complete without added emotional labor.

What changes most noticeably when these qualities are present is the tone of partnership. The relationship feels less like something that must be managed and more like something that can be experienced. Shifts no longer feel threatening. Expression no longer feels binding. Reflection no longer feels like rejection.

For women, this often registers as being met rather than interpreted. There is less need to explain shifts or defend needs. For men, there is less anxiety about losing connection when energy changes.

What is being brought forward is not perfection. It is capacity.

Capacity to stay.
Capacity to listen.
Capacity to wait.
Capacity to engage when engagement fits.
Capacity to let go when release is needed.

These capacities were already trained through the earlier frameworks. This book simply places them into partnership.

When rhythm is respected, relationship stops being a constant test. It becomes a shared process.

Chapter 11

STANDING IN RHYTHM TOGETHER

This book was not written to explain everything. It came from real conversations, lived experience, and curiosity about how people actually move through connection over time. The intent was simple, though not easy: to notice rhythm, respect it, and stay present inside it without trying to control it.

What these chapters explored is not a theory of partnership, but a way of relating. One that acknowledges that both men and women move through phases, that energy shifts, needs change, and that stability does not require sameness at every moment.

For men, this book continues the work begun earlier, not by introducing new practices, but by reinforcing posture. Feeling, awareness, and timing are not ideas to think about. They are capacities that are lived. When a man is able to feel himself, regulate his reactions, and understand when to act and when to hold, he becomes more capable of meeting a partner without overpowering or withdrawing.

For women, this book is an invitation to be seen more clearly in the reality of cyclical experience. It affirms that changes in energy, sensitivity, and expression do not need to be explained away or defended when rhythm is understood. Those shifts are not problems to solve. They are part of how connection breathes.

When both perspectives are present, partnership does not become effortless, but it does become more resilient. Disagreements still happen. Tension still arises. Differences still matter. What changes is that those moments are held within an understanding that allows movement rather than rupture.

Standing in rhythm together does not mean being in sync at all times. It means allowing difference without making it threatening. It means trusting that inward movement is not abandonment and outward expression is not demand. It means staying oriented toward connection even when energy changes.

This work does not end with reading. It shows up in small, ordinary moments. In pauses that are allowed instead of filled. In conversations that unfold rather than rush toward resolution. In choosing restraint when reaction would be easier.

If this book offers anything of value, it is this perspective: partnership works better when it is allowed to breathe. Not perfectly, not constantly, but honestly. From that place, rhythm becomes something shared rather than something endured.

www.ingramcontent.com/pod-product-compliance
Lightning Source LLC
Chambersburg PA
CBHW060705280326
41933CB00012B/2312